CHERISHED WHISPERS

CHERISHED WHISPERS

A Wife's Journey to Reignite Romance

CARMEN WILDE

QuantumQuill Press

CONTENTS

CHAPTER 1

Introduction

This project was born from the deeply common frustration and sorrow experienced by a leftover of us who are married. We miss the romance that was once in our relationships. We find ourselves questioning if we married the identical individuals we dated! Some of us are downright hopeless. We have settled for the nuts and bolts of marriage and try to enjoy our partner, but actually missing the emotional and physical an in depth connection we once shared with them. We miss feeling cherished. Our story is one we've been told from many different couples. It's an important one to share. My husband and I found ourselves living in two completely different worlds. In some ways it seemed we happened to be single parents of our three young children. And in many situations this was true. We were both being equally good parents to our kids, but not being an important other to each other. At the height of our marriage crisis, when each of us felt loss over what to do and where to go, my husband took a unique job that required several months of travel. It was here that we realized what it was we had been missing from one another and found the path to get it again. This was not an easy journey; in fact it took several years and is an ongoing process for us. However, we enjoy a referenced level of happiness we never thought we'd reclaim. Our desire for this plan is that we could give you the steps we took, plus further, to reignite the romance in your relationship.

CHAPTER 2

Understanding the Importance of Romance

"There's just no time" is a poor excuse. People make time for what they consider important. When relationships break down, it's generally due to a lack of time and effort one puts in to understand the other's feelings and needs. Romance often falls in the same category, where one or both spouses don't see it as something that needs scheduling. If you both look back to the dating period, isn't that how your relationship started in the first place? Ever ponder how it slowly and unnoticeably degenerated over time? Ingraining it into your routine can put life into your marriage and say "my spouse is my top priority".

Love is a combination of trust, faith, understanding, and the little day-to-day acts and selfless acts. Love is sustained by action, a pattern of devotion in the things we do for each other every day. It's no secret that those who are in love enjoy doing things together. They might go to a museum, a restaurant, or take a drive in the country - all in an effort to spend quality time. Quality time together is the key ingredient in building an intimate relationship. When you were dating, you were relishing romance; you felt special, thought about nothing else, and had fun. Sadly, for some, they see romance as a chore, an obligation, or a trick to get the spouse to let their guard down so they can get what they want. In reality, it's a vital way to express love. It's more or less reliving the dating period and making your spouse feel special. It's essential in creating a strong bond.

Reflecting on Past Experiences

People have different memories on Valentine's Day. Some are happy, some are sad, some are exciting, and some are just boring. Recalling vivid past experiences is actually good. It helps you remember things you've done, and if you find it happy, you can do those things once more. Those who have happy memories tend to have successful and romantic future Valentine's Day. But sometimes past experiences can bring up psychological problems. This is especially true with a past that involves a difficult romantic relationship. It is easy to doubt whether future attempts at happiness will end in the same way, count on failures learned in today's relationships. But we must remember that we bring joy and affection to relationships, not from the success of our past, but from the current cultivation of our feelings for each other. We often mistake it that we need to obtain something to make ourselves feel like we once did during its time. What you should realize is that obstacles and material are different, absence bears the same results, and innermost desire is what motivates. It's okay to not do something grand. Step right and left with your hands lightly touching. Make an open-hearted dinner and tea for when returning from a walk in the rain. Leave a small note or a humorous random phone message. These little things are acts of love and can make a very different Valentine's Day from that of the past.

This is also a good opportunity to admit past mistakes. Troubles from the past sometimes deviate us from our path. We often do things that hurt others, let alone mistakes. This is the real romance killer. It's easy to simply say it was because I didn't like who I was with, but for humans, we are proud creatures, pointing the finger always brings profit. The truth is that weakness was the cause. To see weakness is to feel failure, to feel failure is to result in further weakness. What we need to realize is that everyone makes mistakes and change is the evidence of repentance. Feeling and dedication may not falter even if the word is lost. Without deep self-reflection, be it alone or with a mate, even minor change will result in no small feat. Now is the time to take back lost romance and change what has hurt others in a positive manner.

CHAPTER 4

Identifying the Challenges in a Marriage

Many difficulties arise in all marriages, stemming from a variety of issues. Some trouble spots are obvious, such as an affair, an addiction, or a major illness. But the most common problems occur when one or both partners develop harmful attitudes or behaviors that damage the relationship. His Needs, Her Needs: Building an Affair-Proof Marriage pinpoints the ten most vital relationship needs to prevent marital breakdown for couples. These are affection, sexual fulfillment, intimate conversation, recreational companionship, honesty and openness, an attractive spouse, financial support, domestic support, family commitment, and admiration. If these are not being met, couples may find they are increasingly distant and feel that they are living with a stranger as they lead separate lives. This has been termed 'apartness' by relationship educator Dr. Lana Staheli which has actually a precursor to separation because the couple becomes more and more disengaged. Staheli also suggests that because couples these days are rushed into a life building a home, they are not necessarily acquiring the necessary skills for communication and problem solving in order to make that home happy. The lack of quality time and difficulty in effective problem solving can also many other issues. The Relationship Matters program offered by The Psychology Foundation of Australia identified the highest ranking issues in families as being communication problems and financial worries, as compared to those without children whose highest ranking issues were life balance and the loss of the relationship with their partner. Additional issues, mainly more of a relationship stress, are the habitual behaviors and attitudes that become detrimental to the success of the love or the marriage. It is often described as a 'pattern of accustomed behavior we follow in our attempt to get our way'. This pattern can become more of a systematic way of bribing, threatening, manipulating and punishing to coerce the partner into giving them what they want. This problem is directly related to the acceptance of incompatibility as when feelings become more negative towards the partner, the level of punishment increases i.e. 'if you loved me you would...' and affairs are more likely to provide a balance of the unmet needs. As with negative feelings leading to the desire to be apart and living with an unmet need in a love bank account decreasing the level of love not only are more arguments and fights initiated, but with a decline in sex too this behavior just becomes a best response. If rewards for bad behavior are not obtainable and each partner feels that any aim to coerce the other has become futile, separation is likely to occur. An example and by far the most damaging to a marriage is domestic violence, which is characterized as the physically violent attempt to perform an act to the partner.

CHAPTER 5

Exploring Communication Strategies

They came up with a metaphor of a funambulist crossing a tight-rope. The funambulist represents a discussion and the tightrope the safe path that leads to resolution of the problem. Usually, when discussions deteriorated, it was because the funambulist veered off the tightrope. Mary provides some examples of ways she helped to keep the funambulist on track. This can be anything from knowing when to take a break if she was getting too emotional, to deciding on a main point that she wanted to address and not letting the topic spread out into minor but related issues.

Mary shares a simple checklist that she found useful when first trying to improve communication with her husband. This involves a shift away from focusing on what she thought her husband should be doing and focusing instead on herself and what she could be doing. She found it helped her to be mindful and non-judgmental. At the core, Paul and Mary's communication struggles were often about the way they were segueing into tough discussions.

In this chapter, Mary shares her story of working on effective communication. A lot of the common advice around "communicating better" wasn't helping her. At the beginning, she examines the advice she was often given about "using 'I' statements". Although on the surface level, it seemed like good advice, she found that it just made her feel disingenuous and frustrated. She shares her experience and her realization that for her, being able to honestly express her feelings was tied to worth and authenticity.

CHAPTER 6

Rediscovering Passion and Intimacy

An important first step to reigniting the spark is to rebuild the friendship between husband and wife. This means spending quality time together without outside distractions. A couple can try reminiscing about happy times together, remembering what they love about one another and what first drew them together. This should help to resolve any negative feelings or tension and can be done in a relaxing environment. Laughing and having fun together is a great way to release any lingering tension and help create a sense of closeness.

Intimacy is an essential key for igniting passion. It encompasses feelings of closeness, connectedness, and being bonded to one another. It is easy to identify a lack of intimacy in a relationship but harder to define the exact cause. Often it is the result of unresolved conflicts and feelings of disconnectedness that have driven a couple apart. In extreme cases, couples may feel more like roommates than husband and wife.

A great way to rekindle intimacy is to engage in a new romantic ritual such as cooking a meal together, giving each other a massage, or taking a bath together. Intimacy has been lost when one or both partners are 'too busy' for one another, so it is important to schedule a regular time for these rituals until they become comfortable. A wife should be patient and give her husband gentle encouragement and stimulus as his positive response to these activities will help encourage more intimacy and physical closeness between the two of them.

Schwehm has made an important point. For a couple to reignite passion and intimacy, it is crucial for them to be open and honest with each other. They need to be willing to try new things and discuss their feelings about the new experiences. This way they can learn about each other's needs and desires and can begin to reintroduce passion and love into their relationship. An open line of communication makes it easier to set a comfortable romantic mood because partners will be more responsive to each other's feelings and will be more connected.

"Attend to how one cultivates and moves creatively in the areas of intimacy. Pay special note to the intriguing aspects of intimacy and try to devise new ways of relating. Explain to your partner what you are doing and give them an opportunity to participate and share themselves in the new way you are creating" (Charlene Schwehm, MSW).

CHAPTER 7

Nurturing Emotional Connection

Now, we cannot fully list every possible purpose or love cry message, but another goal of emotional connectedness is to make the love message and the feeling of love that is experienced and understood here prolific in every behavior. This will boost the net emotional atmosphere of energy in love.

In giving and receiving love, it is important to realize that expressions of love behaviors will make us feel loved and improve emotional connectedness. Similarly, a behavior that is most loving in doing a purpose will also be a cause of much feeling and fulfillment of love. This may be said to fall into the category of helping an auto mechanic work on a car with the purpose of making a repair. When the most fulfilling time comes and the problem is fixed with ease, the mechanic has repaired both himself and the car. He will feel happy and fulfilled. This moment is a moment of love for himself and the car.

Humans hate having their cry messages ignored. They get the feeling that their pain and their need for love is invisible to their partner when advice or a complaint is given in place of a response of understanding. This is a major cause of emotional disconnectedness. So, it is time to give and receive love by listening for cry messages, understanding them, and then responding to them. This can be practiced using CVCC's "Heart to Heart" listening and communication and the "HOPE formula". These are great tools that a couple can use to work at this, making a goal to build and sustain an understanding and love response atmosphere for both present and future cry messages.

A common scenario is one where an individual feels hurt and misunderstood after receiving a complaint. They are crying in their heart for understanding and love, but they only receive more speak and a further complaint. Now, the change of the topic or the defense is the most common tactic for not hearing and not giving the cry message, but it is not desired and will improve emotional connectedness when it is replaced with supported listening and expressions of love.

The response to these cry messages and the sending of them is what we want to work at changing in ourselves, as it will markedly change the love emotional connectedness between partners. Now, many of the love cry messages are responded to in a way that drains love energy out of the emotional atmosphere and does not give the needed love. This is usually an honest response and it is usually a change of the topic of conversation, defending self or other, through denial or a counter complaint or criticism.

Effective communication is a part of it. Communication with an attitude of giving is most helpful. In our day-to-day communications, we send a lot of messages that are really cries for love. These messages usually are a complaint, either overt or covert, or a criticism of self or other, or a cry of pain masked as anger towards self or other. These are the major ways we give messages that we are hurting and need love.

Identify emotional connection between the partners as "The sophisticated process of emotional communication that is required when two individuals experience being under emotional siege from within themselves or each other." They value emotional connectedness and are committed to staying with their partner through thick and thin. This above gives us a benchmark to determine whether they have emotional connectedness. At the right time, it helps us to know where they stand in terms of nurturing it and which ways can be used to improve it.

CHAPTER 8

Embracing Physical Affection

Specific problems may arise concerning touch and physical affection in the relationship. Many women may feel that their husbands touch them only when they want sexual activity and translate this into a feeling that they are only a sex object to their husbands, rather than a person to be loved. If this is the case, it must be realized that sexual activity and affection have not been properly linked, and the husband does not know other ways to show affection. His attempts to reach out to his wife may have been met with rejection, and this was the message that was received. Sexuality may have taken on a meaning of being the only time he truly feels close to his wife, and he may act out all his feelings of nurturance and affection at that time. This is a serious problem and can lead to further problems in the marriage. The establishment of open communication and identification of the various needs for touch and sexual activity are requirements to resolve this. Regular practice of affection and touch without the expectation of sex can lead to the re-establishment of an intimate bond and help both partners understand each other's needs.

Touch is also a way to release sexual tension without always having to focus on intercourse, reminding both partners of the joy of sexuality without the pressure of constantly feeling that it must lead to something else. A hug or a gentle caress can lead to a release of tension and passion that can bond a couple more closely together. And the communication of love and warmth through touch can help keep the fires of love and passion alive throughout the years.

One of the problems that we women face is wrongly believing that men do not have the same emotional needs for affection and nurturance that we have. Men's learning experiences may have been different from ours, and they may express emotions differently, but they do have the same basic needs. Touch is healing. And the gentle and tender touch from his wife may help a man feel lovable and define himself as something other than a success or failure at his job.

In past chapters, we have discussed the importance of beginning to communicate openly with your husband. In verbally expressing love and warmth, the non-demanding ritual of touching and being touched, nurtured and cherished will naturally become part of the relationship. The communication of emotions through touch can take away anxiety and depression and help calm the mind and open the heart to one another.

It is important to realize that physical affection is not merely sexual activity. Physical affection is the use of touch to convey warmth and the genuine love that one person feels for another. It is holding hands, hugging, kissing, a light touch on the arm. It is the simple things which may mean so much.

CHAPTER 9

Creating Meaningful Traditions

Traditions play a big part in keeping relationships alive. They give a sense of belonging and provide security for couples in good times or bad. Simple acts such as an exchange of love notes, or a love code can create feelings of closeness and exhilaration. Holiday celebrations, whether the normal ones such as Valentine's Day or an invented one, can bring couples closer. Take for example the Finnish celebration of St. Knut's Day which is celebrated by going out to the wilderness, on a cold winter's day it might mean a picnic by the fire, in a blanket, in the living room. Anything out of the ordinary done together as a twosome can give a sense of shared experience and knowledge of one another. A tradition should require a special coming together and provide a lasting memory.

Nurturing and maintaining strong relationships takes effort, and there are pleasant symbolic references to that effort. One way to revitalize a relationship is to focus on the positive by creating some cherished memories or treasured experiences. Couples can start by reviewing the early days of their relationship and engage in activities they enjoyed together - sometimes the simplest date can prove the most meaningful. In recalling and repeating a special evening shared together, perhaps an impromptu picnic, a couple can bring back the feelings of romance and carefree enjoyment.

CHAPTER 10

Balancing Responsibilities and Quality Time

This activity in and of itself took several attempts to actually have happen! (Life is so unpredictable sometimes.) But after the first successful attempt, my husband and I were commending one another on a job well done for rescheduling that only took two weeks to finally push through due to life's little detours. This resonated with me that if you are determined to try and find time with your spouse, they will acknowledge it, and that in and of itself can be a special moment.

In my own life, my husband and I would only have half a day on a Saturday to spend together, minus any obligations that could come up. That was when I realized timing and scheduling was the key for finding quality time to spend with each other. I had to keep in mind his schedule, my own schedule, and any special events that would be taking place in the future. I pulled out a calendar and looked at the dates when something would conflict with our usual availability and picked a date that was the least likely to shift because of outside conflicts. We both marked that date and time on our own individual calendars and agreed that barring any emergency or last-minute work conflicts, we would be spending that time together.

We do not always have the luxury of a full day off to spend with our spouses, lazing around and doing whatever you feel like doing. If we are not working, we are usually catching up on housework. If you are not spending time doing housework, you are usually keeping yourself to a schedule to make sure your kids are staying busy with extracurricular activities or their homework. This is sometimes the same schedule that your spouse is keeping themselves to (depending on if they are working or staying home with the kids). Whether it is conscious or not, it is rare that you and your spouse's schedules are perfectly in sync.

CHAPTER 11

Overcoming Setbacks and Difficulties

There are also more specific obstacles to the variety of techniques that can be used. For example, planning outings and doing new things may be hindered by financial restrictions. Bringing home small gifts and tokens of affection can be ruined by bad timing. A woman, when faced with such difficulties, must be creative and resourceful. If money is tight, there are still many things which cost little or nothing and can be fun and different from usual activities. Many impromptu simple events can be the most fun and laughter is a great way to emphasize feelings of love. If timing is bad and things go awry, a woman must simply soldier on and learn to laugh at the unexpected. Hiccups are a part of life and she must not let them discourage her.

Difficulty arises from internal or external sources; there is always a possibility that romance may not be rekindled until it has been thoroughly tested. Having the strength to overcome such trials is imperative. One setback often faced by women attempting to restore romance is that their partner is not responsive to their efforts. This can be incredibly disheartening. They may feel that their partner simply does not care for them anymore, when the reality is that many men simply do not understand what is happening and may even feel resentful at having a previously comfortable relationship disrupted. This can cause tension and hostility between the two parties, which will turn the woman away from her intentions. Here, understanding and determination are needed. As with any minor argument, it is simply something that needs to be worked through. If the woman can persevere with her changes, in time her partner will understand the reasons and become more open, thus leading to a resolution.

CHAPTER 12

Seeking Professional Help and Guidance

Seeking professional help can be expensive, with the NHS also having long waiting lists for patients. However, many find that the benefits gained from therapy are well worth the costs. It is recommended that couples discuss the costs of therapy and inquire about qualifications and experiences in the first session. Remember, therapy is an active process and both partners should be prepared and willing to participate for it to be successful.

When seeking a specialist, ensure you feel comfortable and that the therapist is a fully accredited member of a professional body such as the British Association for Counselling and Psychotherapy (BACP), the College of Sexual and Relationship Therapists (COSRT), Psychology, or Psychiatry. Therapists tend to have different training and approaches regarding sex and sexual problems, so it may be advantageous to search around to find a therapist appropriate for your needs.

Seeking help from the professionals can be one of the most important and useful steps when trying to overcome a sex-related problem or difficulty. Most GPs are comfortable discussing sex and sexual problems, so could be a good place to start. However, seeing a specialist, such as a Relate sex therapist, a psychosexual therapist, or a specialist at a sexual dysfunction clinic, will mean an expert assessment.

CHAPTER 13

Embracing Self-Care and Personal Growth

Self-care helps build and maintain our marriage, preventing the feelings of loneliness and isolation that many wives encounter. When we care for ourselves, we radiate an energy that is uplifting to those around us, and our husbands are naturally drawn back to us. Eileen, a mother of two young children who has been married for 9 years, shares her experience. "Since having my children, I have been very engrossed in my mommy role. I've always been a great believer in attachment parenting, and I've put every ounce of myself into mothering. But I think I've forgotten how to be a wife somewhere along the way. I've ended up feeling quite burnt out and resentful. I can see now that I definitely neglected self-care. I stopped doing the things that made me happy because I told myself that my focus now had to be 100% on my children. After a while, I lost sight of the woman that I used to be. I felt very alone in my marriage, and I think my husband felt the same. I'm still working on fulfilling my own cup, but I have noticed a big difference in my interaction with my kids and my husband. I'm no longer shouting, and I'm more present and playful with my children. My husband and I are laughing together a lot more, and he's started giving me more compliments. I think the biggest thing is that we are actually finding time to talk, just as we used to. Self-care is a habit that I don't intend on breaking again."

An easy way to do this is to pick just 2-3 activities and schedule them into our diaries every month. Treat these appointments with ourselves as though they are a meeting with an important client. This increases the likelihood of follow-through and keeps us accountable. High levels of self-care both prevent and heal many emotional and physical health issues. When our own cups are full, we are more patient, tolerant, and understanding towards our husbands and children. This, in turn, greatly enhances family happiness and reduces unnecessary stress.

Taking time out from our busy lives to sit quietly and reflect is a very powerful tool. For some, this may be through meditation; for others, it may be through prayer. Reflection enables us to reconnect with our inner selves and helps us to get in touch with what makes our hearts sing. Other forms of self-care may include reading, attending a dance class, cooking, writing, painting, yoga, or spending time with friends. As wives, it is important to evaluate what activities we participated in heavily prior to getting married, as these activities are often the first to go once children come along. It is essential to start incorporating some of these back into our lives on a regular basis to help maintain our own happiness.

Chapter 13 discusses embracing self-care and personal growth as crucial components to maintaining a strong marriage. Emerging research suggests that happiness is one of the highest predictors of physical health and longevity. As wives, our ability to experience happiness comes from within, and a big part of our happiness relies on the amount of self-care we give ourselves. Society often teaches us that self-care is an indulgence or a selfish act - this notion is absolutely incorrect. Self-care is the most selfless act a wife can do for her husband and her family. It is the act of refueling our own tanks so that we have more to give and share with others.

CHAPTER 14

Celebrating Milestones and Achievements

Specific events, such as birthdays or anniversaries, offer a chance to reflect on past achievements and plan new ones. Put aside time to speak with your mate on these occasions. Congratulate each other on past successes and discuss what you'd like to achieve by the next milestone. This can be framed as another opportunity to plan for the future and strengthen your relationship while doing so. After some casual conversation, perhaps go out to celebrate and splurge a little on something that you both enjoy. These moments offer a great chance to bond and create lasting memories with your significant other.

We come into this world with a purpose. When we fulfill it, or come closer to fulfillment, we feel fantastic. There are a variety of options for tracking personal progress, be it a simple journal or something more elaborate. Whatever method you prefer, celebrate your achievements, no matter how small. And get your husband involved too. Have him take you out to dinner after you've hit a goal, or exchange small, meaningful gifts. Taking time to celebrate will bring a positive mood into your home, as well as a sense of satisfaction. It'll remind you that as a couple, you're both moving forward.

CHAPTER 15

Sustaining Romance in the Long Run

• Discuss and agree ahead of time, and renew this contract as necessary, that divorce will never be the solution to the difficulties between you. This agreement ensures that you will never consider the "D" word as a way out or a weapon during spats. Making the conscious decision to tidy up the little messes along the way rather than throw the whole marriage away will give you the determination to persevere through the tough times, growing stronger in your commitment each time you emerge from yet another storm.

• Make sure, as life becomes increasingly full with children and commitments, that the couple continues to cherish and nourish their alone time together. Carve out time for a special weekly date. Alternate making the plans and surprise one another. Share your dreams and plans. Keep a journal of your private thoughts and longings, then exchange journals for a secret peek into your mate's soul. Make a marriage scrapbook filled with memorabilia of your times and token gifts to one another. Constantly cultivate your love. Never take it for granted.

CHAPTER 16

Conclusion

But the writing has done more than show a wife how to renew her relationship with her husband. It should have become clear throughout the whole book that people view marriage as a microcosm of life itself. By improving her relationship with her husband, she has improved her life in general, and she has improved his life. They have learned to be more caring, affectionate, assertive, and understanding. They have learned to work through communication rather than make assumptions and judgments. People who have read the story and lessons and vicariously taken journeys of their own will likely experience changes in themselves and their lives. This should make the topic even more relevant now. What is a marriage and what can it be? How can we constantly improve our shared life? These questions, when approached as shown in the writing, become a way to understand and improve upon the human condition in general. The ideal is to live a life always improving and cherishing.

The final offering to the reader offers a full range of considerations for the journey: what has been written, why, and the effect it should have. The reader is not just asked to accept the written words, but to actively do what has been done by the wife and look at the husband in reverse. Look at the situation from the husband's point of view and try to interpret his behavior with the same understanding that she has been given these past months. Place yourself in his shoes and understand that he has used the same understanding for her so far, and gauge his reactions to her advances with a full understanding of assets and liabilities. This means looking at the bumps and bruises that they both have from the past and how these affect their capacity to start again. Always, always concentrate on the assets and attempt to enlarge them. Regard the liabilities as challenges to be overcome.